PARANOI

from Socrates to Joan Collins

Napoleon

Ralph STEADman

Illustrated by Ralph Steadman and published by Harrap

Treasure Island
Robert Louis Stevenson

SCHIZOPHRENIA
"Schizophrenic behaviour is a special strategy that
a person invents in order to live an unliveable situation."

R. D. Laing, The Politics of Experience

PARANOIA
"I wouldn't be paranoid if people didn't pick on me."

Anon

"Just because I'm paranoid doesn't mean to say I'm
not being followed."

Anon

Acknowledgements
Central Television. The study of Paranoids was
used in a documentary two-part series called
Zero Options–A Study in Schizophrenia,
directed by Peter Cannon and David Jones.

The Observer Colour Magazine

PARANOIDS

from Socrates to Joan Collins

Ralph STEADman

HARRAP
LONDON

Dedication

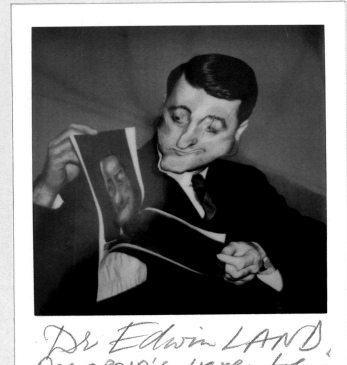

Dr Edwin LAND,
POLAROID'S Inventor
without whom......

First published in Great Britain 1986

by HARRAP LIMITED

19-23 Ludgate Hill, London EC4M 7PD

© Ralph Steadman 1986

ISBN   0-245-54471-2

Designed by Vic Giolitto
Printed in Italy by
Imago Publishing Limited

Contents

Introduction

In a little bay in South-West Turkey called Turkbuku, on a hot Turkish morning after the sun had been up a while, having already taken photos of the sunrise, I made a film, engaging everyone in the village, anyone who was there – and the place was full of Turkish intellectuals from Ankara, they'd all come from Ankara University. I dreamed up an idea on a jetty, in front of our hotel, a little wooden jetty, very crude, and these people used to sit opposite the jetty every day, drinking beer under a shade out of the sun. They went out of the sun because after nine o'clock it was just incredibly hot – and so I managed to get them together. They got quite excited actually, getting up in the morning very early and coming out to do what I had in mind – all they needed was someone to say, 'Well, the idea is this, I want you all out here at six o'clock in the morning and we're going to make this film and we've got this scenario in which someone's going to be raped on the jetty,' very symbolic – that was my idea, you see. I had a little Agfa family movie camera. I stood in the water adjacent to the jetty and filmed them going through the motions, which I had worked out from a storyboard. And there was one lady, a sort of mature beauty of a kind, a painter as well and an artist called Meshtilt. She was Dutch, and she spoke French and she lived in Paris. When she discovered I did drawings, cartoons and the like, she wanted to show me the illustrations that she had done for a series of poems. They were rather beautiful calligraphic images. It was mid morning. I said I'd pop round to her place so she could show them to me and I took with me a Polaroid camera. Why, I'm not really sure. It was very brilliant sunlight – she was living in a little row of white single rooms or apartments and the light permeated the whole room and it was very brilliant. She was wearing a sort of loose dress, a linear thing, so that when she lifted her arms it made flowing white lines, and I thought that was just wonderful. I had to take a picture

of her against the white wall, so I did, and then I said to her, 'Now, I don't want you to just sit there when I take your photograph, I want you to go "Waaaah" with these white lines on the dress going upwards.' Most people go "Waaaah", when you tell them to. I didn't know what it would be like but I wanted to see what happened because the effect was so spectacular. The dress was so loose but at the same time so delineated. I wanted to try to capture that particular quality – 'I want you to go "Waaaah",' I told her again, 'and when you're up there like that I'll be taking the picture before you've finished your action', which is the reason I've always liked to do photography anyway – something between movements. I'd rather catch something going from one movement to another than in repose. In repose you don't find it – a quality you get when people are actually going through a process, a thought that's going to move them from the one attitude to the next in the way of being, you know, the way we are: sometimes thinking thoughtfully and then the next minute we've got an idea so we move – on the point of change, and it's that point of change that one tries to catch in photography because it's possible to freeze a moment. When you draw a caricature, you're looking at that all the time and it's the moment between that you realise you're actually capturing – it's the most life-like part of anybody – the moment of expression – of transition; they're making the full use of their face to express themselves – their inner emotion, although it is unconscious to them. It's a thought, a new idea – that's what makes people reveal themselves. In repose they're acting. It tends to affect a caricature when you draw someone when you just say, 'Would you mind sitting for a minute', and they sit for a minute and they shuffle and they look about and they say, 'Is this OK?' and they look to the side and you say, 'Well, that's OK but don't

continued on p12

CRUDE Beginnings

Sunrise - TURK BUKU

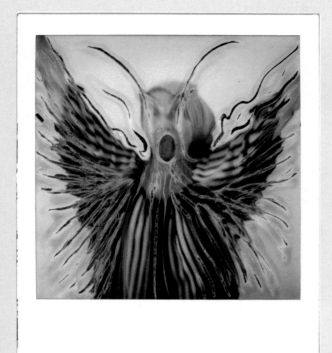

8

Turkish Scene

H.M. The Queen at 60.

Prince ANDREW.

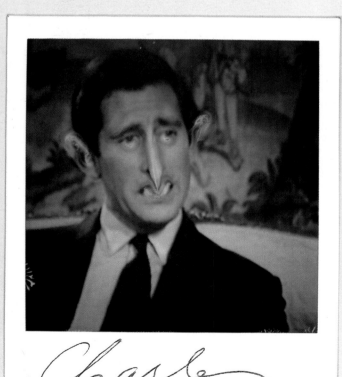

Charles

worry about that, just keep talking to me', so what I want them to do is keep talking because when they're moving their hands, they're expressing themselves and the expression is the thing that's showing on the mouth, on the point of indication, you know, the points of reference, the eyes, the nose and the mouth. It's the combination of those elements that make up the caricature, so if they're just simply in repose, the caricature's just going to be wooden. What it doesn't do is allow people to express their natural characteristics. They might use their front lip a little more than usual so the front lip becomes a part of it. It's just that the lines you're drawing become a little more animated and you're able to move the lip, ignoring the form and emphasising the function.

I digress, but I digress for a reason and that is to help people to understand why you'd even bother to take a picture of someone and then try to change it. I find the best pictures, the best photographs taken of people, have been those in the process of change; that is, the figure has decided to move from one stage to another – and so I made this woman use her dress against the white wall, which was very graphic; the dress was graphic and the facial features were graphic – the face was very brown and interesting with high cheekbones and generally good bone structure – and I made her sit for me through five pictures. I was sitting on one chair and she was sitting against the wall and I just said, 'OK, I don't want you to sit, I want you to move because I'm going to do something with it.' 'What are you going to do?' 'Well, I don't know, I've got a hunch about something – I'm going to use a camera which I haven't used for ages – the Polaroid.' I'd got these films with me and I thought well, let's do something – it all looked so impressive. I knew there was something I wanted to do with them but I wasn't sure what until I walked back to the hotel. The hotel was a room on a block and

continued on p19

The Queen & Prince Philip.

Tutankhamun

Elizabeth I

Queen Victoria

Bishop of DURHAM.

the hotel main part was the bar where you could eat and so forth. It was strong sunlight and I put the films down and left them. They'd already developed, but they looked incredibly gooey and soft. The heat was terrific, so I took one and I marked it with a biro, but the biro leaves a line on the surface of the Polaroid which I didn't want so I got a pencil instead. I started following those lines and I realised that I could make the lines more accentuated – moving the gelatine between the top film and the bottom layer – there are two layers and between them is a soft layer of gelatine which was expanding in the heat so that for a while it remained malleable and you could push it around. What you're doing is pushing around a light-motivated material which is still in the process of change. It's as if you started off with a perfect blueprint of someone which you could then alter according to your needs. It's almost like saying well, pity I haven't got them in a three-quarter view, which may have been what I wanted – but how can I change it; or, it's a pity I haven't got them with their eyes a bit wider or with a smile; or, a pity I shouldn't turn them round so I could see their noses a bit more clearly or whatever ... it's a pity it's not quite right so I'd like to take another one of you but you'll have to wait through however long it takes. So, with this, I was moving this stuff and it was beginning to change but at first it was a bit angled; that is, I was just moving into the lines on the woman's dress and it was just like scoring it but then I thought I'd see what I could do with the face because it was still developing. It wasn't that I thought, hey I've got a good idea – let me start playing with this and see if I can push the gelatine around ... that didn't occur. It was just that it was all so plastic, I could push it with my fingers, it was so soft – that's what gave me the idea – it was so soft that I could squeeze it and the features on the face changed.

Buddha

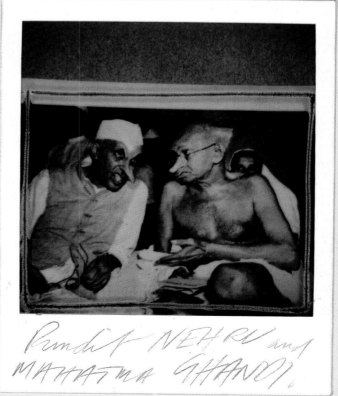

Pundit NEHRU and MAHATMA GHANDI.

continued on p22

19

The Virgin Mary.

Christ!

21

I was very excited because this was a breakthrough for me. There have been various attempts to make a Polaroid into a painting but has anyone else ever thought of using it for a caricature? I don't know ... could it move like that, or is it destroyed as you start moving it because it sort of self-destructs? So, I started playing with the nose on a three-quarter view and I knew that the idea was working and I knew it would work again when I was able to pull the woman's nose out over the edge of her cheek in a three-quarter view and still leave the impression of the nose that was in the original photograph. It actually convinced me that her nose was that long. I realised that it could be done. Once you know you can pull something, after that it is just a question of how far you can pull it before it starts to self-destruct and you can't go any further.

Then I started doing the people in the café. Some of the pictures were crude because what I was doing was adding colour where it started to break down. I was faking it and it wasn't working, but then I tried a sunrise and I thought, what can I do with that? You know, the sun comes up, can I change a landscape? – and I did one with a sun just coming over the horizon – very still – and then all I had to do with that one was to make a squiggly line down the water area and it looked extraordinary, yet it was still real and believable, so that became a guideline. If you change the pictures so that they become impossibly contrived, they lose the reality. I found the best ones, the ones that worked the most, were the ones that still convinced me that it was the real person and you'd just photographed them – those were the best. But sometimes the aesthetic side of the movement – where lovely things happen in the gelatine with the mixture, between the two surfaces – becomes important. You realise there's another area to work in. You don't just simply do a Polaroid and move it slightly – that

Dr Runcey – Archbishop of Canterbury

The Pope

continued on p28

maggie

maggie

maggie

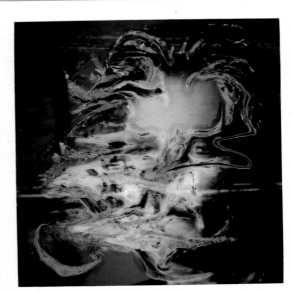

maggie

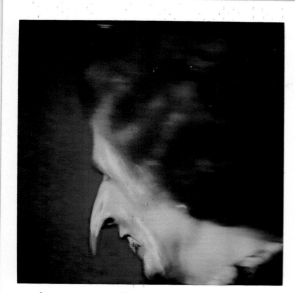

maggie

maggie -

Maggie

maggie

Sir Robin Day

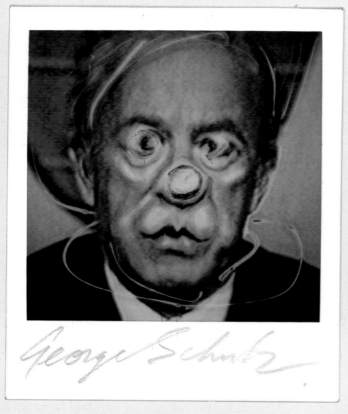

George Schulz

James Schlesinger.

is the basic approach, but there's another way and that is to turn it into a painting, you know, give people a sense of another dimension using the Polaroid as the basis for your painting and, bear in mind, that if you were to take one of those Polaroids and blow it up to six feet square on a canvas and repaint it – as a portrait – it would be wonderful.

I started taking things from television at the Tory Party Conference when I couldn't get near Maggie Thatcher. It was a commission from the *Observer* Colour Magazine. They rang me up when we got back from Turkey. I got this call from John Tennant, the Art Director, and he said would I like to go to Blackpool and draw the Tory Party Conference, the delegates. I said, 'No, it's too boring, I couldn't do it,' but I thought of Paranoids. I said, 'I can do Paranoids for you, and he said, 'What's that?' and I said, 'Well, Paranoids are a sort of Polaroid. I work on them and turn them into caricatures. It depends on the photographs I take but it does work in more cases than not' – so John said, 'All right, sounds funny, can you send me some', so I sent him some 35mm slides and he said, 'Yes, let's go with it, but we need a writer'. I said, 'Well, what about Hunter S. Thompson?' and I gave him the number and he tried but apparently he couldn't reach him – he was in San Francisco or somewhere. Instead, they got Russell Davies, the link man for *Saturday Night Review* on the BBC, and we met in the lobby of the Conference Hall. I'd already done two or three pictures of people, using the flash bar on the Polaroid to give me sufficient light. There was me, an accredited photographer with a Polaroid – they thought I was nuts. People looked at me strangely – obviously not a bona fide, just some freak who got a pass from somewhere. It's that sort of feeling that you get. An outsider – I always was. If you've got a string of Nikons around your neck and Christ knows what else, and you've got a big bag full of colour film and spare lenses, then people will look at you and think – 'OK, he's a professional, let him go.' But all I had was this Polaroid in my hand and that's it and you go 'Bzzzz, Bonk' and then something comes out of the end and you rush away, get yourself a coffee and go into a corner with it and then start scratching away at it – people notice that kind of behaviour. There was a piece that appeared in the *Mail* that mentioned a raving scruffy-looking bastard who was wandering around the place taking Polaroid pictures and turning them into the most gruesome portraits. I think people humoured me actually. Once or twice I got a wonderful opportunity to take a picture of someone and my bloody flash didn't work – it's awful – taking a picture of someone and they think it has been taken, assuming that the people who take the pictures know what they're doing, so if the flash doesn't go off, it's obviously an adjustable camera that can take a picture without any exposure or whatever, so it worked – 'All photographers are like that, aren't they, even the dummy with a Polaroid – who knows?' I couldn't say, 'Oh, the flash didn't work, can I take it again?' – so unprofessional. I was the only one who knew that what I'd got was a piece of black Polaroid and nothing else.

Gadafi.

I couldn't get anywhere near Maggie Thatcher. So, never mind, I thought, look, I could do some of them like this and some through the closed-circuit T.V. When I got Rhodes Boyson in person, he was so pleased that the Press was following him but his picture turned out to be like the Elephant Man. It was still a bit crude. I was still driving the films too hard, working at them too soon, doing all the things that you do when you're nervous because you've got to go back to the *Observer* at the end of the week and they're going to say, 'Well, where are they?', and all you've got are a bunch of things that are scratched out and

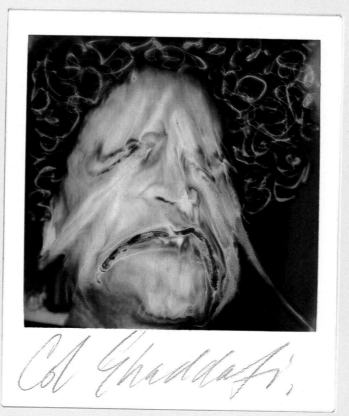

Col Ghaddafi,

continued on p38

Mobutu of ZAIRE.

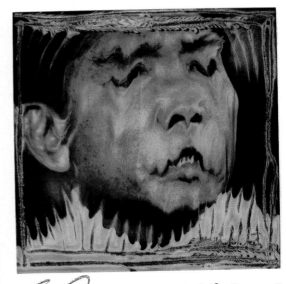

Ex-President MARCOS.

BOTHA.

Bishop TUTU.

Casper Weinberger.

KURT
Dr. v. Waldheim.
Austrian President.

Adolf

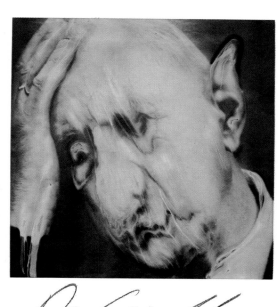

De Gaulle

Jeffrey ARCHER

Keir HARDIE

J.F. Kennedy

Winston CHURCHILL plays ORSON WELLES.

opposite Roosevelt

hopeless and too weird to publish. They had to be developed in such a way as to convince others that what they are looking at was practically a photograph but not quite. The important thing was that it had changed – it wasn't just a straight photograph any more – it was something entirely different, and it was a new way of caricature and it was quick. Lightning sketches are quick but not quite as convincing as these lightning photographs of people. Someone on the promenade in Brighton does a quick sketch but it's not really me, hardly an impression, but when it's a photograph and you do something to it and it still looks like you then it's time to worry. If it looks bad, which is what I call the most important part of it really, for the camera never lies, they can't really disagree with you. I was using a piece of machinery which people must take seriously, which in our present day and age they can recognise and relate to. Admissible evidence in any court of law. If there is a photograph of you with an axe in your hand – then you're guilty.

It is only a more forceful form of political cartooning, if it *is* really an unforgivable assault on someone's personality or character, and not a comment on their policies. It's not like a political cartoon where the elements of a situation are portrayed and the character is put into that situation expressing the predicament of his attitude or whatever for good or ill – it's not that at all. It's a portrait of the person as if they were sitting for you and what you've managed to do is reveal something. Sometimes the photograph is that good that you can change the features of the face to add another or uncover another layer of the person's character and you've shown them to be what they are – that's what you're doing – you're pulling away something, you're either dragging the skin around or even uncovering it or being a little more aggressive and diggin

continued on p42

Karl MARX.

Lenin

Mao-Tse TUNG.

Marshall TITO.

Mr WINNIE MANDELA

George WASHINGTON

Richard NIXON

in so you make a more linear expression of their features. Then, I started taking things from television. I couldn't possibly visit everyone with the flash behaving erratically – pointing it at them and nothing happening – so I found that the TV monitor was incredibly clear so I went to it and just took a picture and went away to see what happened and of course it worked. I thought since I wouldn't get anywhere near these people and do what I wanted without inhibition, being a coward at heart, it was even better, and I was able to take ten, a whole pack, of Polaroids of that one person giving his speech and I knew that I had him for at least half an hour. I would stand there watching the monitor screen with people watching me wondering what the hell I was doing, taking pictures from the screen. Knowing I was Press but obviously doing something unusual. I would just say it was a new secret process – 'I can't talk about it, sorry.' I'd put the pictures away – 'I can't show you, not now.' So it was obviously secretive and it got picked up by a couple of people, journalists, who said 'What the hell are you doing?' – why was there someone here with a Polaroid camera – it was worrying. I felt a bit like someone who was really trying to find a place to plant a bomb – and security was rife – the place was black with police.

In fact the Polaroid camera is used by professionals just to see if they've got the lighting right but they would never consider using it for a finished picture. They get out their Haselblads to take the picture. They have Polaroid backs for Haselblads now so they can get it coming through the lens. So, that was what was happening and I was really spending a lot of time in the bar with these Polaroid creatures, developing, taking a little longer over some of them – I would take about six and go away, believing I only had five minutes to draw into them before they even properly

continued on p45

Ayatollah Khomeini.

Charlie CHAPLIN

developed. Then I realised that wasn't the way. I had to wait, because the film gets a certain glutinous quality later and starts to tighten up after about ten or fifteen minutes and then you've got a stronger surface to play with and it really becomes tight plastic which you pull around. It's like half-soft plasticine when it's really working. It is the face of the person when you begin but it is still mobile. I found that if I warmed it in a pocket next to my heart I could extend the process. This is the important thing. The flexibility, the opportunity to keep changing it and maintain some sort of likeness. It is practically three-dimensional like clay, you can move it with your hands. With these Polaroids you can pull them a certain amount and still maintain a likeness but after a while you can lose it because you do actually get to the point where the gelatine will not move any further and what happens then is it just goes dead on you, not just fixed but dead. You have pushed all the gelatine too far and you can't bring it back.

I realised what was most important about that exercise at the Blackpool Conference was that you could use machinery and nothing but machinery to get your caricatures. It was machinery telling machinery what it wanted to know, which was 'I need a picture of Maggie Thatcher – if she comes on the screen, I can photograph it because the right light input will be projected for the camera, it will register on the film, and I will have an image sufficient to work on and make into something else.' You don't have to go all over the world photographing people in person – you can simply do it through the television camera, and in fact make it that much more valid, because we live in this age of media and television. We can transmit images of anybody, anywhere all over the world – the only reason we know so many people is because it's transmitted electronically – it's not because we've seen

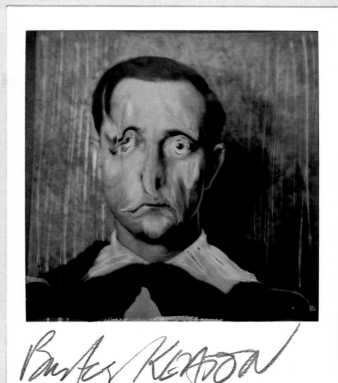

continued on p50

Cagney

James Cagney.

Fred Astaire

them and when you see them in the flesh, you often think you know them. They are strangers but they're not strangers through the box so that became a valid point to make.

I think the process will probably continue to evolve. There's a ten by eight camera and there is a six foot one and it takes a full-size shot. But I think the size would prove too big to work effectively. I would have to use a broom handle.

My camera went wrong in front of Jeffrey Archer so I rushed out and bought a new one with an S/600 film and it doesn't work – it hasn't got the gelatine in it. They've managed to improve it, to make it almost one surface – good for holiday snaps but at the same time, no good for art. Perfect for the person who demands perfection. Hopeless for the dabbling amateur like myself.

Ralph Steadman, interviewed 6 June 1986

Fred Astaire

Ever since man realised that he could scrape an image on a wall and create a likeness of a fellow human being, he has been fascinated by the possibilities of the portrait – and those he portrays have shown an equal fascination and sometimes fear of the result. For many, the capturing of a likeness, however rudimentary, has exercised a power over the subject.

In many cases the portrait or symbolic image has fed an already stressed mind with an indefinable fear for which a term was invented in the mid-nineteenth century – a term which by its very nature may be describing an imagined disease – something which does not even exist. The word 'paranoia' was coined by a German psychologist, Karl Kahlbaun, to describe an uncertain condition whereby a patient suffered persistent delusions of grandeur and persecution, imagining himself to be under political surveillance by persons unknown or even a dear friend referred to as 'they'. An historic figure often features as a model to someone with delusions of grandeur when they believe that they are that person. Often it is Napoleon or Jesus Christ. Maybe Napoleon thought he was Alexander the Great or Messalina so maybe that condition is not without its uses if you are an artist. We are all paranoid. It is a natural condition or at least a universal one, otherwise we would not have reached the stage in the military game known as Star Wars. We are riddled with it and in spite of rational platitudes from a multitude of sources, we are likely to continue nurturing our paranoia because in many ways it is a creative thing. Without it many of us would be redundant. Artists, musicians, writers and generals would be inactive and moribund. They rely on their fantasies to fire and fertilise an otherwise dormant lump known as creative energy.

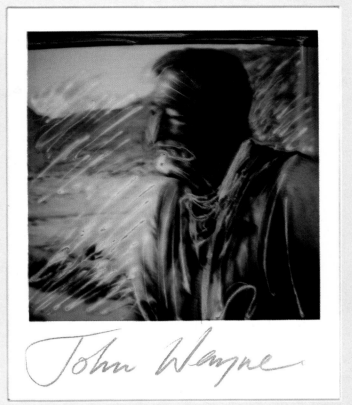

John Wayne

Katherine HEPBURN.

continued on p59

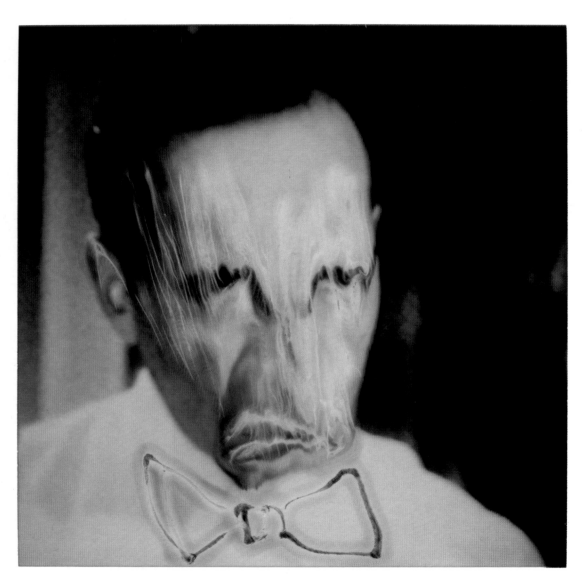

Woody Allen.

Yul Brynner

Vivien LEIGH

Meryl STREEP.

Greta GARBO.

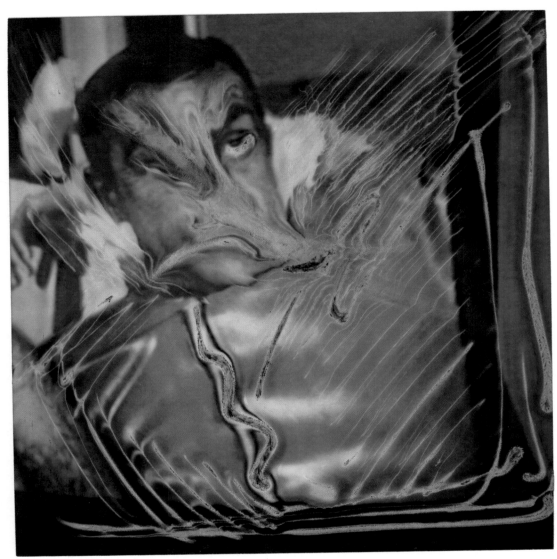

Sean Connery
James Bond.

Julie Andrews

Elisabeth TAYLOR

Lawrence OLIVIER.

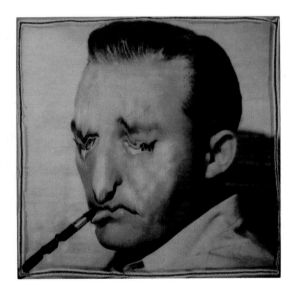

Bing CROSBY.

Apart from the personal ego battle between Freud and Jung, there was another problem of incompatibility between the two of them. Freud believed that the neurosis or mental problem of a patient was best cauterised from the mind by his 'talking cure' whereby a patient talked out in words of 'free association' the core of his problem, the suppressed truth, whether it be a forbidden wish or a horrific experience best forgotten.

Sooner or later the patient is forced to face and speak the words he was trying to suppress. Reluctantly, he releases them as an escape route or safety valve – once opened the release becomes a flood and, in a sense, the patient is 'cured'.

Jung believed that perhaps it would be a better path if the patient were taught to live with his problem, believing that it may well be a source of creative energy, particularly in a creative person. We may need our neuroses to function. We may even realise that possibility intuitively and feed these neuroses to induce the necessary state of mind to perform.

Everybody does something to their day to construct some pattern that makes working moments bearable. Some use the clock, arriving at nine and leaving at five, even by choice, and some practise Zen at 6am, then perform wonders till noon. Others walk the dog before breakfast and still catch the 8.10 to Paddington, and some pedal themselves silly on a stationary bike for 20 minutes before drinking a pint of orange juice and devouring six eggs Benedict on rye toast before entering a boardroom full of similar people who prefer their eggs sunny side up and their bikes mobile.

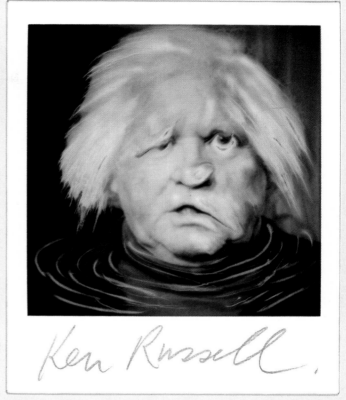

Ken Russell.

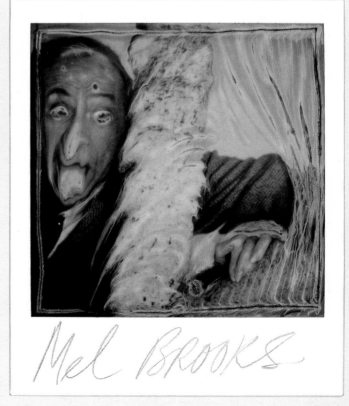

Mel BROOKS.

continued on p61

David Puttnam

It is a structure, self-imposed, but it allows the practitioner to caress his neurosis, his insecurity, his paranoia. It will get him through the day. The successful victim of his own paranoia is the one who believes in his method. His structure. The structure that helps him to cope with the certain knowledge that minority groups are secretly organising a campaign against him, are recording his every move and that 'they' are trying to retard the growth of his children!

These are random examples but they are typical of the paranoiac's fears and they have imposed a presence in the mind which at the time is real enough.

So don't worry if you think you are Nefertiti, or the Sun King – you probably could be if circumstances were different but that's not really the point.

The point is that believing yourself to be a fantastic character is your bid to be immortal, to live forever. So what's unhealthy about that?

It seems to me a sight more unhealthy to believe that there is life after death and millions do that – but nobody says they are sick. Just religious, and full of hope.

In 1955, T. Adeoye Lambo made a study of paranoiac psychoses in the Yoruba tribe – an African tribe from Nigeria.

Adeoye Lambo reveals the reason for his interest and the relevance of his study. He states that there is no better approach than to study the gradual, historical evolution of the psychiatric concept in other cultures and quotes a colleague (B N Jana 1953) that medicine as it is known and taught today is largely concerned with disease in the civilised white man. When the world is considered as a

Sir Peter Hall
as DIRECTOR.

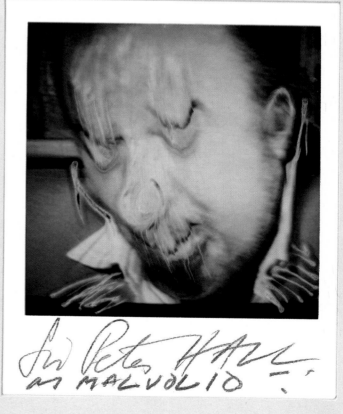

Sir Peter Hall
as MALVOLIO

continued on p67

Lawrence Olivier
as OTHELLO

opposite Clint Eastwood

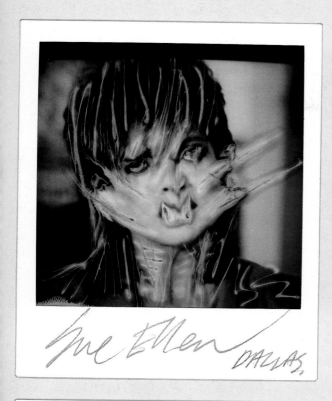

Sue Ellen DALLAS.

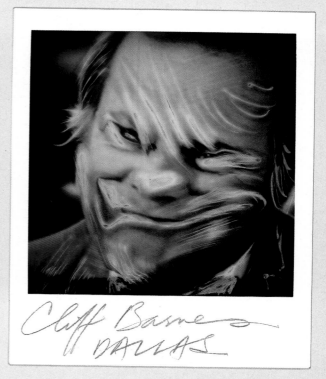

Cliff Barnes DALLAS

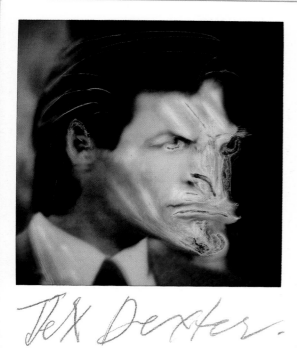

Tex Dexter.

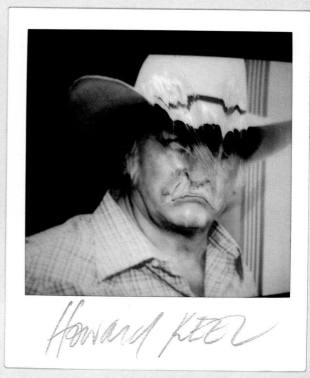

Howard KEEL

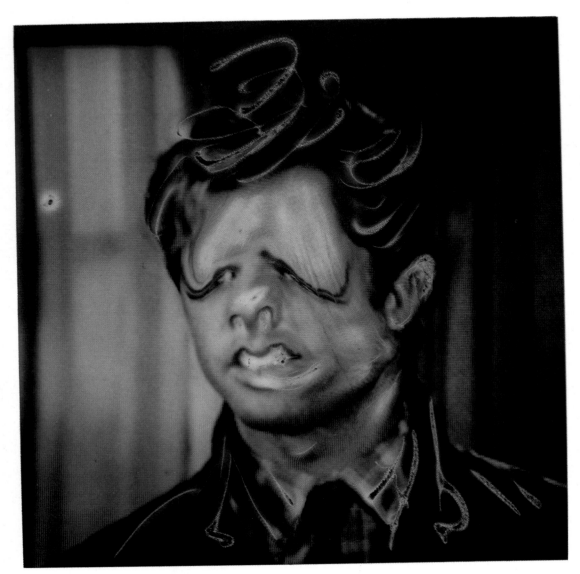

Miles Colbn.

whole the white men are a minority group and civilised man is a recent phenomenon of history. The study of little-known races living in primitive environments is medically unexplored territory and can be expected to reveal manifestations of disease, if not new diseases, which may well prove important in the general advance of medical knowledge. I considered the egocentric nature of the white man, particularly the western white man and his various activities. They can hardly be considered sane, and appear to be gathering momentum. More sinister yet, those activities seem to be induced and augmented by a state of mind closer to paranoia than to objective or rational thought. Dr Lambo relates four case histories, the first of which had a conclusion that cannot possibly be surprising. It is also not so foreign in nature that we cannot see a parallel with western society today and I include all of those who consider themselves to be upright, respectable citizens. We all practise, unwittingly perhaps, psychological warfare on others, mainly because of our own insecurities and the pressures put upon us by our ruthless pursuit of ambitious goals. Dr Lambo's story goes, and I quote at length:

Barbara STANWYCK corbmy.

"The patient was seen by me three weeks after the onset of her illness. She was still confused, excited and grossly aurally hallucinated. She was hearing the crying of many children. She was naked and was walking about the room in a very anxious, apprehensive manner, but without any co-ordination of purpose or movements. The phase of the illness was one of mental confusion during which she was incoherent in her speech, excited and acutely hallucinated. After her relatives refused to have her admitted into the Asylum at Abeokuta, she was sedated.

After the initial state of excitement and confusion she was still manifesting symptoms of the acute stage but it was obvious that the

Barbara STANWYCK.

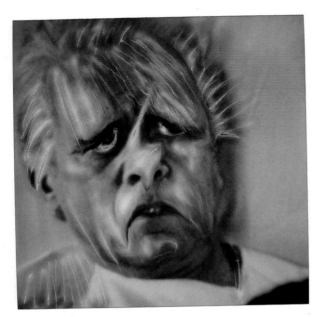

Blake Carrington.

illness had entered a new phase. When she was seen on the sixth day her confusion had abated considerably but she was anxious and her emotion was one of lability.* She was incapable of giving a good account of herself, except for her complaints of her womb – 'my children are in there'. Her behaviour at some periods could be said to have been based on the fundamental pattern of hysteria. She was convinced that some people were persecuting her and conspiring to 'drain her womb' of its contents. She could feel movements in her womb and her illness, according to her, was due to the fact that the vaginal passage was blocked by the effect of a native medicine. After a week she still remained in this state of mixed psychoneurotic-psychotic state, with no other evidence of the basic features of any known psychosis.

Her relatives were co-operative and gave the history of the patient. The family history was clear of mental and nervous disease. Her mother had had seven children, five of whom were alive – three women and two men, married with children. The patient's pre-psychotic personality was good – a quiet but sociable person. She was of a mixed body build.

Her husband said that the patient had been worried for a very long time over her inability to have children. They had done everything possible but no pregnancy seemed to be forthcoming. They had paid a lot of money to the native medicine men of various cults and they had themselves made several sacrifices to the gods and ancestors. When her husband became apprehensive, though sympathetic, he 'married' another wife who later had children by him. The third wife came in 1948 and had already had one child. Although the first wife (the patient) still kept her place and played the role of the first wife, she nevertheless became jealous of the procreative ability of the co-wives.

*From labia – pertaining to the lips. She was talkative.

In October 1950, she started to report the movements of the co-wives to their husband. She complained that one of the co-wives was using native medicine against her because she was having bad dreams about her. The husband investigated this allegation but found it groundless. By December 1950 she incorporated her husband into her delusional system and later was able to persuade her own relations to believe her ideas of influence and persecution. She thought her husband was trying to get rid of her because of her inability to have children.

The husband further elaborated on the central core of the psychogenesis* of this illness by revealing that as far back as 1944 he could remember her getting restless and worried over an incident. It was revealed that the patient lost her 'asu Osu'** after putting it outside to dry in the sun. Her suspicion that somebody might have taken it for magical purposes was confirmed when after many years she found that she had failed to have children. The second wife, who had two children by her husband, was a local girl and after she came the patient thought that the co-wife's parents must have been responsible for taking her 'piece of menstrual cloth' so that when she had failed to procreate, their daughter could usurp her position. Thus the patient built up a plausible system of ideas. The patient later confirmed what her husband said about her illness but entreated me to 'open' her womb and to release her children.

On further enquiry, it was found that she had missed her menstrual periods for over a year but 'her pregnancy was suppressed' by some magico-mystical power of the 'evil-doer'.

Physical examination was negative. The abdominal examination was quite unsatisfactory. The patient did not allow

* Fundamental reasons for mental state.

** This is the term used for the piece of cloth that native women used for their monthly periods. These pieces of cloth are usually washed and kept from month to month and guarded very closely for fear of being taken by an enemy who might prevent them from having children or even kill them.

Fallon Colby.

Sable Colby.

continued on p74

Bau Cont my NAME

Bob Geldof

ELVIS PRESLEY.

Early Dylan

Paul McCastney.

Ringo

palpation* and every effort to conduct any pelvic examination (per vaginal route) was met with hysterical outbursts because of suspicion. On my advice she was removed to Abeokuta General Hospital where she was examined under anaesthetics and fibroid was tentatively diagnosed.

Two days after the examination, the patient manifested a florid picture of paranoid schizophrenia**. Her prior vague symptom depersonalisation (she thought she had changed and become 'inexistent' since her menstrual cloth was lost), ideas of persecution (of psychogenic origin), and auditory hallucinations (voices of other women saying that she would not live to bear the children in her womb) became well-established.

It had been revealed here that prior to the development of her illness there had been self-reference tendencies of a mild nature. These self-reference tendencies became intense in the acute stage of the disease when only a few pathoplastic*** features were apparent.

By the middle of February 1952, pathoplastic features became more pronounced and could easily be studied. Recurrent confusional states (her abdominal 'movements' acted as a trigger point) characterised by perplexity, hallucinations of magico-mystical nature, and hysterical hypomanic behaviour completely dominated the clinical picture, while the basic schizophrenic features seemed once more to be clinically quiescent or screened. Not only did the pathoplastic features nullify the intensity of the basic schizophrenic features but the entire symptomatology became less intense and much more vague.

A study of the symptomatology of all the phases of the psychosis revealed a number of central aspects of her emotional life, within the

* Examination by touch.

** Indeterminate mid stage. Not yet a certifiable schizoid.

*** Imagined bodily states.

continued on p78

John LENNON

George Harrison

John + YOKO.

Brian EPSTEIN.

David BOWIE

Mick Jagger

Jimi HENDRIX

tribal social expectation. Due to the existence of a primary anxiety the content of her delusion was coloured in this sense. The pathoplastic features seemed to be a purely functional attempt to keep certain affective occurrences out of consciousness.

It should be added here that fibroids (though relatively rare) are a well-known cause of psychiatric disturbances in the native women. This patient was later removed to another village to see a medicine man and the writer was never allowed to follow her up. All attempts at hospitalisation were unsuccessful.

This patient, after three years in the village, is now reported to have been admitted to Yaba Mental Hospital, Lagos, and the clinical picture is one of clear-cut chronic paranoid schizophrenia."

It is not surprising that the poor woman went quite mad – it would have had the same effect on me – you don't have to be a doctor to see the logic in the development. Her experiences, to say the least, were extreme and wretched.

During our lives we all suffer unpleasant experiences, balanced hopefully by happy ones, and those experiences sow the seeds of our pet paranoias to a greater or lesser extent. Nothing to worry about at all. I use the above example to illustrate why I claim that we are all paranoiac, should anyone protest. Our various and milder forms of paranoia adjust to concepts within the reality of our world and what we have to suffer as a part of it. To western man, reality is the endeavour to master things. In more primitive cultures and in the Third World, reality is in the origin of the soul, an acquiescence on a spiritual level with the forces of nature, man's relation to his

Boy GEORGE

continued on p80

Pete Townshend.

Sting

community and its social members and *of their* relation to the spiritual world. The American Indian has always maintained that the white man is finished because he doesn't believe in anything any more and in that he may be right. If it doesn't come out of a tap or a packet, it obviously doesn't exist. However, the fact that we may all be suffering from paranoia at all is proof enough that the spiritual side of our natures is still kicking somewhere deep in the bowels of our 'self' and whilst we may no longer look to the State-controlled Church for spiritual guidance, it may as well hang around just in case the need arises for some kind of religious revival. For that trip, we are going to need to report back to Mission Control for orchestration.

It's when you're a bum and paranoid that the personal tragedy erupts, not when you're a world leader, or even a bank-manager. They're allowed to be paranoid because that's their job. When you are a down and out, and you think you are Attila the Hun, people laugh at you and lock you up. You are a problem sane and a sore on society. That's bad enough. But if you start making claims that you are here to save the world from depravity and your name is Mahatma Gandhi, then you are not only a problem but you may also be an anarchist and therefore you must be interned in a mental institution called a prison.

Society cannot deal with the abnormal unless it is in terms which they can recognise as 'contained'!

We prefer our politicians mad because we elected them and we want our money's worth. And anyway, it's official so anything is allowed so long as it has the stamp of approval which we wrought with a big cross. We complain bitterly and long to retract our vote, but that's not the game, so we pick on the most visible

continued on p83

Rupert Murdoch

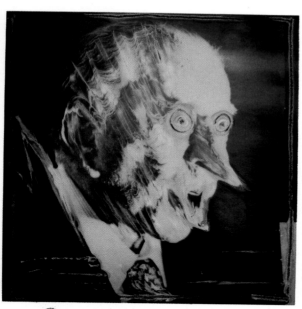

Paul GETTY.

Richard BRANSON.

aspects of our most visible leaders and accentuate and distort them in order to laugh at them. The art of caricature has always been applauded because it allows us to laugh at our faults and mistakes in others. We continually look for opportunities to display our faults by finding the same faults in them. It has the effect of relieving the mental pressure and the awkward sense of self. Most people, I find, respond quite positively with laughter to a picture of themselves which has distorted their features but remains a likeness. It is acceptable because it allows them to air their preoccupations with themselves and yet remain unspoken about. Genuine physical deformities are, of course, another matter, and they remain taboo, I would say, and it serves no purpose whatsoever to laugh at the legs on a cripple, unless the cripple laughs first. The lucky ones amongst us have manageable deformities and acknowledging them visually makes healthier fellow-beings of us all. It can be both entertaining and therapeutic. Oddly, it is the ones who have been left out who seem to feel affronted and they are made aware of their own paranoia, though not intended, when their own deformities are not so much ignored but left undone.

Paranoia is a potent combination of fear, knowledge and control, and many people, aware of certain preoccupations within themselves, channel these into obsessions. The fear within drives the knowledge which manifests itself outwardly in acts ranging through musical masterpieces, monumental sculptures, architectural flights of fancy, great novels, exquisite pictures and the founding of empires to something as mean and degrading as rape.

Tragically, there exists an attitude towards paranoia from which we all suffer, but which most of us hide behind a relatively 'normal' façade. This attitude concerns the official

continued on p104

Duke Ellington

Paul TORTELIE.

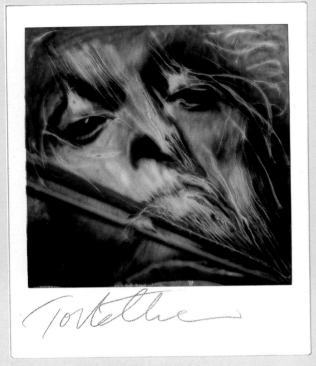

Tortellie

Paul Tortellie

Tortellie

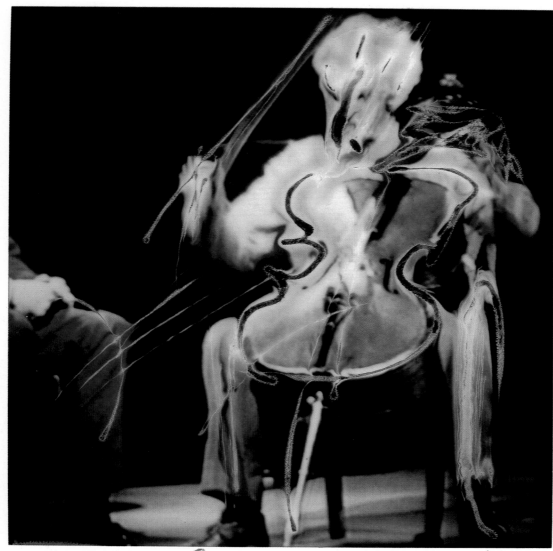

Paul Gotelie

Bach

Julian BREAM
CHURCHILIAN AUTHORITY

Dame Margot FONTEYN.

Nureyev

Sarah BERNHARDT.

Marcel MARCEAU.

Terry Wogan 1

2

3

4

Rembrandt

for FRANCIS BACON
Prophet of the PARANOID.

William BLAKE

Marcel DUCHAMP.

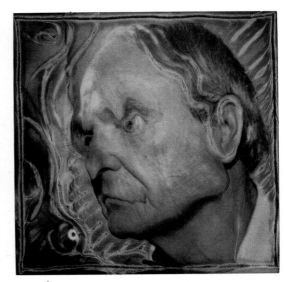

Henry MOORE

Henri MATISSE

Leonardo daVINCI.
after '/. LEONARDO'.

Leonardo da VINCI
in YOUTH.

Michelangelo.

Leonardo da VINCI
at 63.

Michelangelo.

Bertrand Russell

Sigmund FREUD

charge of paranoia upon a person or persons which once made and registered disqualifies what the 'paranoiac' actually says, in his own defence.

The status of paranoia denies a person the rights of rational redress against those who feel qualified to pass judgement.

There is no rationality allowed or acknowledged after judgement has been passed even though most doctors would agree that registered paranoiacs show, and I quote, a relative absence of dementia and of thought disorder. That paranoiacs show little personality disintegration, highly systematized delusions and the absence of hallucinations. That paranoia is a distortion rather than a morbid process, i.e. 'a morbidly transformed expression of natural emotions of the human heart' (Kraepelin).

Some distinguished authorities claim that paranoia if it exists at all is so rare as to be disregardable and if that statement isn't evidence of official medical paranoia then fifteen distinguished authorities are following me in black plastic macs and they want to get me.

'They' have invented something which doesn't exist – a real imagined disease and I know that they are trying to catch me out so that I can be locked inside an institution. But they won't catch me out because they do not know who I am today. And if I am not the same person as I was yesterday then they can't make it stick. They need a body, not just a mind to prefer charges, so my advice to all paranoiacs is to keep on the move. If you are a different person every day, no administration can keep up with you. If we all adopted this approach to life, society would be delightfully unmanageable but exquisitely euphoric, for it would release in all of us the imprisoned souls of our secret lives.

Sigmund FREUD

continued on p110

Socrate r.

Sam Becket

opposite Homer

Solzhenitsyn

Paranoia has been invented by a society, all societies, to impose control on the misfits who appear to threaten and undermine the forces of reason within a hard-core establishment.

That may sound like my own paranoia, but minorities, of any persuasion, which include most of us, want only to be allowed to do what we would wish with our lives in a perfect world – the rest want only to prevent us.

The monster we create to watch over us is the only paranoiac who is truly criminal – the voyeur of the Orwellian nightmare.

Given that human nature stinks sometimes suggests that it also smells sweetly at other times, but the monster that we have invented guards the stink within us. We are what we have wrought. We are stuck with a monster we have created because we are paranoiacs – mean paranoiacs.

We will not provide the air for those who cannot breathe.

We would rather dream of freedom and live by cant and dogma. We are probably right. It is more manageable, but only just.

The true paranoiacs function by being themselves, which may be someone else entirely, but that is the miraculous safety valve that nature has given to us.

However, we choose to live by another order and prefer our actors on the stage contained in their wildness and locked inside the attitudes which are preferably displayed by a goldfish in a glass bowl.

Franz KAFKA

The trout-faced leeches of our official organisations would do well to bear in mind that the main reason we have not been faced with more serious social crises than we have suffered already is because most people are more good-natured and tolerant than they are given credit for. It is not because of any policies of containment devised by planners and organisers that this is so. *We*, the hub of society, prefer to use our paranoia to good effect and live in another world for most of our lives, and let those who would scheme and designate go scheme and designate, and leave the rest of us to be whoever we dare to be.

And anyway, who might you be – are you on the side of the controller or the controlled?

Are you placing people in a category which reduces their condition to one of symptomatic status? For those of you who doubt that they are paranoiac at all, here is a check list:

Are they laughing at me?
I am so happy – but it can't last.
Why is it fine when everyone else goes on holiday?
When I buy a car, why is he selling it?
Did I leave the gas on?
Why do people keep finishing my sentences?
How do you know exactly what I am thinking?
I am guilty and I think they know.
What is that pain in my left arm and which side is my heart?
Oh, God, who is that on the phone?
Is that drunk going to sit next to me and start talking?
Is this lift going to stop suddenly between floors?

continued on p112

Evelyn WAUGH

Is that an echo of my own footsteps?
For a moment I thought – but it's only an old coat on the back of the door.
Is that faint whiff of body odour me?
It is probably him but it may still be me as well.
I can smell burning!
It's the toast – but just check I didn't leave the fan heater too near the curtains.
Faugh! dear!! Who's trodden in something?
(instinctively lift own foot and look at sole)

Which category are they going to put me into – I *know* that is what they are planning, but they won't catch me out because I'm smarter than they think, and anyway if they are one of the controllers they are probably dumb enough to follow rules without question, and anyone who does that prefers not to think too much at all, because if they did they would realise the nature of their own paranoia.

They will also realise that someone is watching *them* for signs of disloyalty, incompetence, confusion and lack of enthusiasm, waiting for them to crack, numbering their days and training somebody else to fill their place.

It's worse when you've got more to lose, those with longer service, unable to start again and more likely to slip.

We are paranoid about our health – when we have our health, we worry how long it will last – did that last drink too many damage my liver? – the aches and pains of everyday life cause paranoia – delusions of sickness – romantic notions of heroic death – mostly unfounded – but of course quite possibly right in some cases – the possibility feeds the fear which is the paranoia.

Paranoia may well be disregardable because we all suffer from it – it is the natural torment of a half-healthy mind at work because we are undoubtedly half-sick too. We may even worry

Ezra POUND

because we are not bothered at present. That's often the time that disaster strikes.

So the mind picks up that quivering thought of possibility and dwells on it, inventing and then replacing complacency with the scenarios of possible developments in our future.

If only we were allowed from birth to develop truly as ourselves. Were we not moulded by the conformity impressed upon us by well-meaning parents or otherwise, it might be possible for some of us to escape the personality-bending process altogether and develop as a neurosis-free human being – so far, a mythical creature.

Unfortunately, or perhaps fortunately, no single set of parents or single person has the skill to detect and interpret the complex make-up of an emerging individual. The pure internal map of genetic structure that even before displaying the programme of a future personality contains the fundamental indications which determine that the emerging creature will be human at all, not to mention male or female.

The psychic movements within us are, to a greater or lesser degree, moulded by external forces and interrupted in their natural flow by the imposition of restraint and redirection.

Generally, a sad lot for all of us. Doomed to a life of paranoiac uncertainty. The genetic formula that makes us what we are has been tampered with and reprogrammed to suit those whose task it has become to protect and love us. That mother knows best when it comes to dealing with our fundamental needs is pretty well undeniable, but before that, response to and interaction with an emerging individual is a guessing game and can only at best be dependent upon the 'guiding' person's own knowledge of self and general experience of life.

Dylan THOMAS.

Oscar WILDE

continued on p117

Norman Mailer

Virginia Woolf.

Zandra Rhodes

There are no experts because we are all the result of the same initial process of damning formation, and lest ye think otherwise, we should remember that to claim that is to claim perfection and that would never do.

Take another good look at yourself. Examine your self-confidence and complacency. Are you proud of what you are doing in this world? Do you feel that what you do is a genuine contribution to society? Is God really watching over you and would he pick you up in a crisis? Can you really say that you are a good person? Have you taken your Valium today, and worse, have you brought them with you?

Don't worry. Being a paranoiac is belonging to a vast fraternity of fellow-sufferers. We are suffering from life and we are gaining in rich association with it.

There is no grand plan. What you do individually is neither here nor there. Nobody is marking up the score. We are a blissful accident wandering around in a black void. There is no one but us. We are alone. We are brothers and sisters pretending a reason for all our actions, hoping for some reaction. We are on course.

When the day of judgement comes who will *you* be? Accept your paranoia as a blessing from brutal mother nature and be your wildest dream. It is there for our salvation. We were not meant to be rational constantly. If we were, we would have blown up long ago at the dawn of our existence.

Maybe someone *is* watching over us, and if we believe that, isn't that being paranoiac?

continued on p118

Norman Parkinson

We are being watched by some big thing in the sky and we don't know what it even looks like. Maybe if we did we would be more paranoiac than we are already. We might really have cause to worry. Better not know, eh, and carry on as before.

I think someone is trying to stop me writing this book because I can't think of anything else to say. And that's another trick they play on you to undermine your confidence. They give you more space than you need and you dry up with the mere thought of filling it. Call somebody, someone, and tell them I'm in trouble – but don't tell them where I live. Tell them I live in Stratford upon Avon and I can't stop writing plays about kings and fools and scheming harlots.

If they want me I may be someone else when they arrive. I will be in disguise. I may have a begging bowl, a long tweed overcoat grimed with city life and countless disappointments held close to my body with a cracked leather belt – and I'll be on the move. I must keep on the move. Someone is following me, or was, but I think they will again. There's always someone, somewhere....What was that?!

Norman Parkinson

Bruce Oldfield

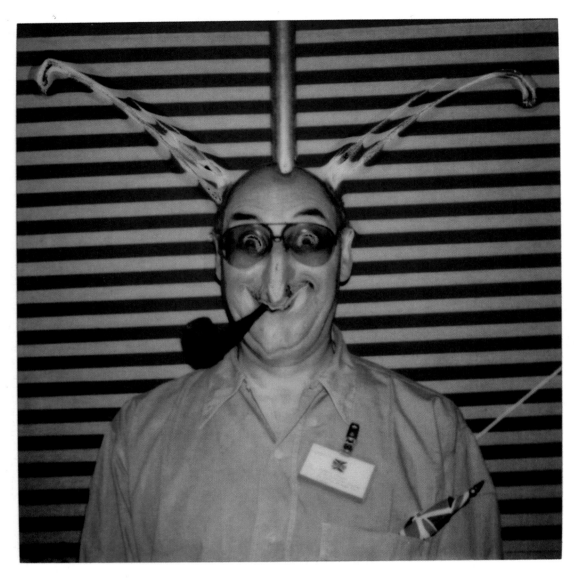

Rodney COOPER
DESIGNER of PIER 4 at HEATHROW

120

Paranoids: A Study

2

3

4

5

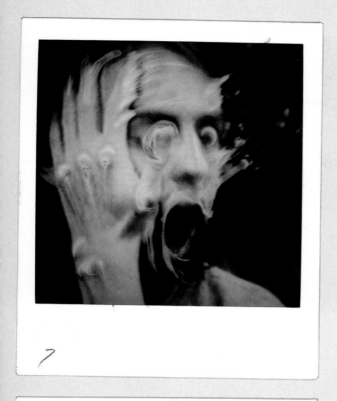

7

8

9

11

Let there be LIGHT

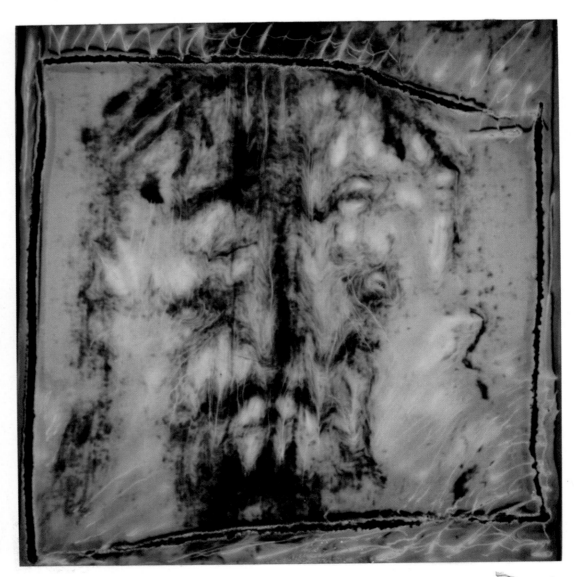

GOD with
Ten Faces

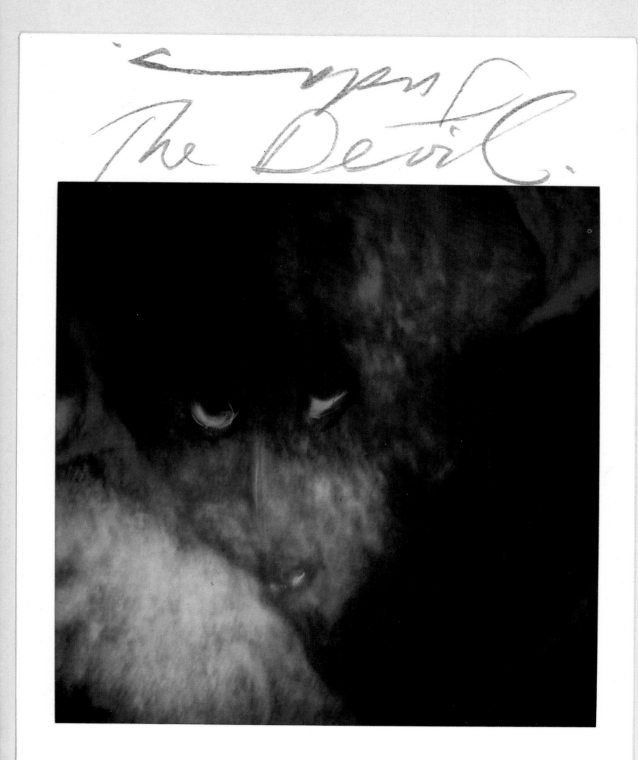

The Devil.

Adam + Eve

The FINAL DEMAND.

Apologies...to those who would have been

Owing to various difficulties, situations beyond my control, geographic and/or agricultural obstructions, including the odd hideous portrayal, not to mention confines of space, I was unable to include the following personalities .....

Boadicea
Ronnie Corbett
Descartes
Virgil
Madame Curie
George Michael
Charles Dickens
Monty of Alamein
Baudelaire
Boris Karloff
George Burns
Marco Polo
Robin Hood
Roger Bannister
Isambard
   Kingdom Brunel
Tina Turner
Malcolm X
Sir Edmund Hillary
Les Patterson
W.G. Grace
Nell Gwynn
Krupp
Donald Campbell
Robert Redford
Emily Pankhurst
Walt Disney
Marie Lloyd
Eric von Stroheim
Marconi
King Arthur
Anne Bancroft
Oliver Cromwell
Daffey Duck
Prince Michael
   of Moldavia
Michael Jackson
Zeus
Christopher Reeve
Kaiser Wilhelm
Freddie Trueman
Christine Keeler
Willie Whitelaw
George Bernard
   Shaw
Millie
Rod Stewart
Florence Nightingale
Rasputin
Rajiv Gandhi
Richard Pryor
Paul Newman
The Merrie Men
Joan Rivers
Christopher
   Columbus
Albert Einstein
Ernie Wise
Haile Selassie
Beethoven

Attila the Hun
Terry Wogan again
Madonna
Old Father Time
Sir Keith Joseph
Bob Marley
Nancy Mitford
Sir Isaac Newton
Abraham Lincoln
June Whitfield
Sheikh Yamani
Alan Coren
Pythagoras
Phyllis Diller
Leslie Crowther
Mary Queen of Scots
Liberace
King Solomon
Noddy
Johnny Carson
Babe Ruth
Rudyard Kipling
Angela Rippon
Jimmy Carter
Sir Robert Maxwell
Anthony Burgess
Marianne Faithfull
Arnold Trubshawe
ABBA
Abraham
Dr. Jekyll
Tallulah Bankhead
William
   the Conqueror
Dr. Samuel Johnson
Tarzan
Rimbaud I
Rambo II
Rin Tin Tin
King John
Mohammed Ali
Aristotle Onassis
The Supremes
Julius Caesar
Bugs Bunny
Owain Glyn Dwr
Marc Chagall
Louis Pasteur
Paul Raymond
Richard Burton
Alice Liddell
Havelock Ellis
Paul Daniels
David Livingstone
Kevin Nebbins
The Queen Mother
Joseph Heller
Arlene Dahl
Fatty Arbuckle
Martin Luther King

Aga Khan III
Alfred Adler
Barbara Hepworth
Alastair Burnet (Sir)
Houdini
Eugène Ionesco
Galileo
Milton Friedman
Cardinal Richelieu
Ezra Pound
Nancy Reagan
Gary Player
Max Planck
   (Quantum)
Edgar Allan Poe
Samuel Plimsoll
Puccini
Tsar Nicholas II
Joseph McCarthy
President Sadat
George Sand
The 4th Earl
   of Sandwich
Spencer Tracy
Mantovani
Xaviera Hollander
Anais Nin
Conrad Veidt
Emlyn Williams
John Belusham
P.G. Wodehouse
Maureen O'Hara
Sir Henry Wood
Jayne Mansfield
William Wordsworth
Andres Segovia
Dr. Albert Schweitzer
Doris Day
Dostoevsky
Jacques Cousteau
Ella Fitzgerald
Noel Coward
Mamie Van Doren
The Smother
   Brothers
Cher
Graham Greene
Arthur Rubinstein
Nelly Sachs
David Lloyd George
Pamela Manson
   (artist's model)
El Greco
Edward Heath
James Joyce
Nikita Khrushchev
Ku Klux Klan
Orville Wright
Ted Willis
Eamonn Andrews

Brahms
The Prophet Elijah
Maria Callas
Géricault
Sir Arthur
   Conan Doyle
Bernadette Devlin
Henry V
Henry James
Søren Kierkegaard
Michael Winner
Tom Stoppard
Billie Jean King
Gustav Holst
Field Marshal
   Slim
Winslow Homer
John Smith
Abel Gance
Alfred Lord
   Tennyson
Germaine Greer
Schubert
Peter O'Toole
Manfred von
   Richthofen
John Bloom
Myra Hindley
Gregory Peck
Jack Jones
The Marquis
   of Queensberry
Werner von Braun
Bertolt Brecht
Colette
Karl Benz
Billy Connolly
Ingmar Bergman
Mikhail Glinka
John D. Rockefeller
Marlene Dietrich
Rip Van Winkle
Henri Cartier-
   Bresson
Ginger Rogers
Marty Wilde
Pablo Casals
Dora Bryan
Arthur
   Schopenhauer
Lisa Minnelli
Gogol
Victor Mature
Paul Gauguin
Carmen Miranda
Groucho Marx
St. Matthew
The Brothers Grimm
Engelbert
   Humperdinck

Sid Vicious
Roald Dahl
Tony Stratton-Smith
The Angel Gabriel
Voltaire
Mike Read
Zeno
Lester Piggott
George Frideric
   Handel
Tom Wolfe
Gerhart Hauptmann
Gracie Fields
Lewis Carroll
Daphne du Maurier
Moby Dick
Alice Cooper
Catherine Cookson
Yehudi Menuhin
Ingrid Bergman
Paula Yates
Tolstoy
Bernard Crick
Lulu
Edna O'Brien
John Dryden
Alexandre Dumas
Ralph Waldo
   Emerson
Bud Flanagan
Ian Botham
Ludwik Zamenhof
Denis Healey
King Hussein
Henry Lamb
Joan Plowright
Ignace Henri Fantin-
   Latour
Dan Archer
Beryl Bainbridge
Kiki Dee
Lyndon B. Johnson
Linda Ronstadt
Ben Jonson
John the Baptist
Barbara Cartland
Carl Gustav Jung
Immanuel Kant
Enoch Powell
André Previn
Leo Sayer
James Stewart
Paul Cézanne
Cardinal Wolsey
John Ruskin
Bill Cosby
Ben Hur
Anthony Quinn
Johnny Hodges
Aaron Copland

Philip Roth
Vita Sackville-West
Cyd Charisse
Gore Vidal
Emanuel Shinwell
Moses
Kate Bush
Samson
Thomas More
Paul Gallico
Italo Zvevo
Errol Flynn
Christiaan Huygens
   (Lenses)
The Kray Brothers
Hans Holbein
Jean Anouilh
Gary Cooper
Busby Berkeley
Lassie
Arnold Palmer
Thomas Edison
Cheeta
Bernard Lovell
Amy Johnson
Laura Ashley
Charles Bronson
Dusty Springfield
Wilfred Owen
Mandy Rice-Davies
Hegel
Arthur Negus
Heinrich Heine
Wally Fawkes
Rudi Kleenex
Admiral Jellicoe
Dr. Kinsey
Elton John
Tariq Ali
Neil Kinnock
Thomas Hardy
Josef Goebbels
Sandie Shaw
Stanley Baldwin
Stanley Matthews
Agatha Christie
John Wesley
John Calvin Coolidge
Diaghilev
Emily Dickinson
Jan Pauli
Washington Irving
Dr. Hunter
   S. Thompson
Lord Haw Haw
Bianca Jagger
Eric Dobby
Simon Scott
Tim Pearce
Judy Fereday .....

..... and one or two others too numerous to mention.